# Conversations on the way

## All-age dramas on Bible themes

# Conversations on the way

## All-age dramas on Bible themes

## TIM STOREY

First published 2001 by
KEVIN MAYHEW LTD
Buxhall
Stowmarket
Suffolk 1P14 3BW

9 8 7 6 5 4 3 2 1 0

ISBN  1 84003 730 X
Catalogue Number  1500427

Cover design by Jonathan Stroulger
Edited and typeset by Elisabeth Bates

Printed in Great Britain

# Contents

# Introduction

'We need some drama!' – the shout goes up. Many churches have found the benefit of using drama of one kind or another in church services. Drama can add a new dimension which often speaks in ways far more powerful than a sermon. Using drama, though, creates its own problems – props, lighting, voice projection and, not least, getting volunteers to learn pages of scripts.

*Conversations on the Way* is a collection of scripts written for a variety of services, including family services, youth services and a Lent course. The main aim was to produce a set of scripts that were either short and therefore easy to learn or, as important, consisted of conversations that could be simply read, allowing the two or more 'actors' a chance to be familiar with the script but able to have it on a reading desk or music stand in front of them. The sketches in this collection were all performed using this idea and they have been used in church, in halls and on local radio.

*Conversations on the Way* takes its name from the conversation that Jesus had with the two disciples on the road to Emmaus. Luke tells us that Jesus started with Moses and the prophets and explained how they looked forward to the very day on which this conversation was taking place. I feel sure that the two disciples had questions and the journey was accompanied by a series of conversations between one who understood and two who didn't. The sketches in this book often contain a character who understands a particular concept and another who is struggling with it.

My hope is that those who read these sketches, those who perform them and those who listen to the finished result will find them an encouragement on their own journey and a guide towards a greater understanding of the One with whom they walk.

TIM STOREY

# How you might use this book

One of the key differences between things Jesus taught and the teaching of other Rabbis was that Jesus taught about ideas rather than a set of rules. When he summed up the whole of Moses' law in one word – 'love', he laid the foundations of a way of thinking that required people to engage their brain, to grapple with concepts that would define the Kingdom of God in positive terms rather than rules that would define it negatively. He used parables to try and convey these concepts, leaving the listeners to draw their own conclusions rather than spelling it out to them. But it is not always straightforward – we know that even the disciples had to have the concept of the parable of the sower explained further in Luke 8:9.

The sketches in this book are not intended to replace talks or sermons; they aim to illuminate stories and parables that people may have heard only once or a hundred times before, by giving them a different or contemporary slant. Some of them were used in youth services in the knowledge that many listening had never heard the story before. In such services, a pattern of use grew up that involved *introducing* the concept through the sketch, *reading* the passage in the Bible and finally *applying* the concept through a talk.

For example, a service looking at our need to keep close to God day by day might include a section containing the sketch 'The branch line', introducing the idea that a railway line will only grow in use if it is part of a network and involves mutual reliance and openness. The sketch could then be followed with a reading from John 15. This could be done 'straight' or using *The Dramatic Bible* or, as is increasingly possible, using a computer Bible to split the reading into parts for different voices to read. The talk could then explore these ideas further, for example, applying them to the need for the Christian community to be dependent upon Jesus whilst being open to each other. The ideas could be further enhanced visually with an OHP projecting a picture of a tree, or running a video in the background. The latter needs to be chosen carefully – on one occasion, the video camera was set on a tripod to film a tree on a sunny, windy day and the result was effective as it added ideas of flexibility, strength and life to the talk. However, on another occasion, a video illustrating teamwork accompanying 'The Body of Christ' proved to be a distraction to a 90-year-old lady who confessed afterwards that she had missed much of what the speaker had said because she was enjoying the football on the video!

The majority of the sketches were originally performed by two people at the front of the church with minimal props and a limited amount of rehearsal time. David Woodhurst and Paul Carter were two willing volunteers (sometimes, anyway!) in a church in Bath. They helped to make the sketches come alive with enthusiasm and a willingness to enter the characters involved. Each of the sketches in this book has a section entitled 'How you might use this . . .' which contains suggestions as to how the script could be used to better effect; and 'Questions you might like to think about . . .' which are intended to stimulate discussion and further thoughts beyond the sketch. These are only suggestions and are intended to encourage the user to be adventurous and creative in their use. So, be *creative*, be *adventurous* and, above all, *enjoy* them!

# HOW IT ALL BEGAN

# In the beginning

*This is a poem making the simplest of points about creation: that if there is no God, then a mind-boggling number of coincidences must have happened to make it all come about.*

**How you might use it . . .**

This is best read in a dark environment with slides of space and the earth projected in the background (these are often available for loan at places such as Diocesan Resources Centres).

In the beginning was nothing,
and no one said anything
and nothing happened.

Then later on
something must have happened
and a couple of hydrogen atoms
who had been getting on quite well
bumped into an oxygen atom
and decided to form a partnership
called 'Water plc' – 'plc' standing for 'potential living culture'.

And then after a few billion years
and a primordial soup
and a billion, billion, billion total coincidences
and an evolutionary something or other
out popped a human being.

Quite remarkable really.

Well,
actually,
totally impossible.

A few grammes of chemicals
and a whole lot of water
and *something* came to be,

something that no one can see,
no one can touch,
and no one can deny:

a soul.

A long way from a beginning

when there was nothing,
and no one said anything
and nothing happened.

**Questions you might like to think about . . .**

- Before there was something, there was nothing . . . so where did God come from?

- If Creation happened because God decided it should happen, how much has happened since then just 'by chance' . . . or is everything planned in advance by God?

- If the writer of Genesis had understood all that we now know about the universe in which we live, what changes would he or she have made?

# The other story of the Garden of Eden

*The Bible tells us that God looked at everything he had made and saw that it was 'good'. He then made people and I am sure he knew it wouldn't be long before they messed it up. So what if God had decided it was too big a risk to let them loose on the good thing he had made . . .*

**How you might use it . . .**

As with 'In the beginning', this is best read in a dark environment with slides projected in the background. The slide show might begin with views of space, the earth and a garden, before moving on to slides of fences, gates, padlocks and graves. A word of warning: be careful what you photograph – the author came close to being arrested for photographing a factory security fence with some very sensitive guards on hand!

And behold, the Lord God looked at his creation
and it was very good.

He looked at the sun and the moon and the stars,
he looked at the seas and the fish,
he looked at the mountains and the valleys,
he looked at the vast array of creatures, small and large,
he looked at the plants and the vegetation,
and, behold, it was very good.

And as the Lord God walked in the beautiful garden
he looked at the man he had made,
and he looked at the woman he had made
and thought,
'How long will it take you to mess all of this up?'

And so the Lord God spoke to the man and the woman and said,
'Because you two cannot be trusted –
if I turn my back for a minute
you'll be eating the apples that you shouldn't

and, before long, you will be cutting down trees
and killing animals that you don't need to
and will have turned this place of perfection
into a wasteland.

Because of all this
I am going to install a set of security cameras.
I am going to arrange for hourly patrols of angels
and I am going to insist that you do not take any decision
without it being in writing
and left with my personal secretary forty-eight hours before it is acted on.
I made this place perfect – and I want it to stay that way.'

And so the Lord God left the man and the woman in the garden
where, for an eternity, they lived happily
without any cares or responsibilities
and without any ability or desire to choose between right and wrong.

And somewhere in heaven
the book that was to be written
containing the stories of people
such as Cain and Abel, Moses, Elijah, David, Isaiah
and a host of others –
remained unwritten,
and the wondrous story of their failures
and their discoveries of God's love for them
was never heard
for it could never happen.

And the need, too, for God to send his only Son
to put the situation straight
well, that was never required.

The Lord God knew the man and the woman
he had created could not be trusted
with the precious gift they had been given,

and so his creation became a cold empty toy

and somehow it wasn't good any more.

**Questions you might like to think about . . .**

- Did God know that the serpent was going to trick Adam and Eve, or did God just hope they wouldn't give in to temptation?

- Is our 'free will' to choose between right and wrong a blessing or a curse? Would it be a better world if we were programmed to always do the right thing?

- If God had stopped short of making people, sticking with the universe and animals, what sort of world would it be?

# If God exists . . .

*This sketch moves on from the simple statement made in 'In the beginning':
believing that Creation happened by chance is just as far-fetched as believing
in a Creator. Here, the question is – what if this massive creation is simply
all there is and we are just here by chance and, worst of all, on our own?*

## How you might use it . . .

This is another sketch that works well with slides of space and the world
in which we live projected in the background. The two actors could stand
with solitary lights on them in an otherwise darkened room, and not too
far apart so that there is communication between them. The sketch
requires the actors to have a reasonable amount of rehearsal time in
order to gain an awareness of the timing for some of the lines.

**A**      In the beginning, God created the heavens and the earth.

**B**      God.

**A**      God.

**B**      The 'old geezer on a cloud' –

**A**      if it helps you to see him that way.

**B**      Or her.

**A**      God must be big

**B**      if God exists.

        *(Pause)*

**A**      But if he

**B**      or she

**A**      doesn't exist

**B** then we look pretty stupid.

 *(Pause as they look at each other)*

**A** And so do *you*

 *(Pause as they look at congregation)*

**B** and so do all the people in the Bible

**A** and down the years since

**B** who said that God exists.

 *(Pause)*

**A** If God doesn't exist

**B** then all this happened by chance:

**A** rivers and mountains

**B** sea and land

**A** birds and animals

**B** all

**A** by

**B** chance.

 *(Pause)*

**A** If,

**B** on the other hand,

**A** God *does* exist

**B** then all of this must have been planned.

**A** It must have been designed with care

**B** and designed for a purpose.

*(Pause)*

**A** But if God doesn't exist

**B** it must all be a waste of time.

*(Pause)*

**A** If God doesn't exist

**B** then we're on our own

**A** sitting on a great big bit of rock

**B** zooming round in space –

**A** on our own

**B** going nowhere in particular.

*(Pause)*

**A** If God doesn't exist

**B** then no one is in charge

**A** no one is running the show –

**B** we're on our own.

*(Pause)*

**A** If God exists

**B** then there is hope.

*(Pause)*

**A** If God doesn't exist

**B** there is no hope.

*(Pause)*

**A**    I believe in God.

**B**    I believe in God.

**A**    It's scary to think what life would be like if I didn't.

### Questions you might like to think about . . .

- If God does exist, is he, or she, on the outside or on the inside of what 'he' has made? Whatever the answer, what is the relationship?
- If God is in charge, why doesn't he intervene more actively in day-to-day life?
- If God designed the world for a purpose, does that purpose extend to individuals — and what might that purpose be?

# JESUS

# Just a bloke

*Most people, given the choice, would agree that Jesus was a good bloke who did and said good things – but no more than that. This sketch is by way of an introduction to the challenge 'Just a bloke?' and aims to bring many different aspects of the question into play in a short time. Ultimately we come back to the question of whether Jesus was telling the truth or whether he was a liar and a fraud – but this sketch starts at the point where many people come from: Jesus as just a bloke.*

**How you might use it . . .**

This could be performed by two people, standing side by side, facing the audience and resolutely not looking at each other or it could be used as a face-to-face conversation (in the style of Mel Smith and Griff Rhys-Jones). The sketch requires reading at a reasonable speed and, if in the style of Smith/Jones, the last line could be delivered with both actors turning to face the audience.

**A**      Jesus.

**B**      Jesus.

**A**      Just a bloke.

**B**      Just a bloke.

**A**      A good bloke, though.

**B**      Yeah, a good bloke.

**A**      But just a bloke.

**B**      Yeah, just a bloke.

         *(Pause)*

**A**      Did some good things.

**B**      Said some good things.

**A**   Good bloke.

**B**   Good bloke.

**A**   Made a lot of people better.

**B**   Blind people.

**A**   Sick people.

**B**   Deaf people.

**A**   Old people.

**B**   Young people.

**A**   Dead people.

**B**   *Dead* people?

**A**   Yeah, dead people.

**B**   *(Disbelieving) Dead* people?

   *(Pause)*

**A**   Good bloke, though.

**B**   Yeah, good bloke.

**A**   Did some good things.

**B**   Said some good things.

**A**   Said we should love each other.

**B**   Said we should forgive each other.

**A**   Said he was the Light.

**B**   Said he was a Shepherd.

**A**   Said he was the Way.

**B**    The Truth.

**A**    And the Life.

**B**    Said he was a Gate.

**A**    Said some funny things.

**B**    Just a bloke, though.

**A**    Good bloke.

**B**    Yeah, a good bloke.

*(Pause)*

**A**    They killed him, though.

**B**    Funny that.

**A**    Not funny, just sad.

**B**    No, not funny – strange.

**A**    Good bloke.

**B**    Helped people.

**A**    Said good things.

**B**    But they killed him.

**A**    Good bloke.

**B**    But they killed him.

**A**    They say he came back to life.

**B**    Who does?

**A**    His friends.

**B**    Yeah . . . lots of people do.

**A**      Bloke down our road does.

**B**      Couldn't have done – just a bloke.

**A**      No . . . just a bloke.

**B**      Good bloke.

**A**      Good bloke.

**B**      Coming back from the dead?

**A**      Just a bloke?

**B**      Just a bloke?

**A/B**  Never!

**Questions you might like to think about . . .**
- Often people ask if Jesus was mad, bad or God – what evidence is there for each of these options?
- People talk about Jesus as a 'bloke' – what sort of a bloke was he? How 'normal' was he?
- Was Jesus preoccupied with God to the point that he talked about nothing else? If not, what sort of things would he have been interested in? Where did God his Father fit into these things?

# Crimewatch

*Based on the TV series 'Crimewatch', this sketch needs to be read in a firm and confident style – even with an impression of one of the Crimewatch presenters!*

## How you might use it . . .

The basic prop for this sketch is a desk. The actor can either sit behind it and act in a very 'officious' manner or could perch on the side of it with the script on a clipboard. An OHP acetate with the word Crimewatch and a suitable 'wanted' picture (for example, the picture of Jesus portrayed as Che Guevara) would help people to understand the concept quickly. A second OHP with the Bible quote (Luke 4:18) could be projected, as well as a third, again with the picture, but with the last line of the sketch as the only text on it.

### *Do you know this man?*

About 2000 years ago, this man, Jesus of Nazareth, was seen in the area of Israel for a period of around three years using aliases including Jesus Christ, Son of Man, Son of God.

This man, aged about 33, is wanted for alleged fraud having claimed to have come back from the dead.

His cover story is that he was on a divine mission having come to earth, as he put it, to 'proclaim freedom for prisoners and recovery of sight for the blind, and to release the oppressed'.

Because of this, police also want to interview him about conspiracy to aid escaping prisoners.

There is also evidence that this man was seen talking to many people – and engaging in unauthorised healing work.

He is reported to have disappeared although reports of his activities continue to this day. Indeed, his gang is very active and it has now grown into a world-wide organisation.

Do you know this man? – the truth police want to hear from you.

Is he who he says he is, or is he a fraudster?

We'll be waiting for your call and so will he.

**Questions you might like to think about . . .**
- Why did the authorities see Jesus as dangerous? Was he a threat to them?
- Do people see Jesus as dangerous today? If not, why not? If so, why?
- What was Jesus' mission? Was it to die on a cross? If so, when in his life did he realise it?

# THE LORD'S PRAYER

# Whose Father?

*The most commonly used prayer in the whole world is the one that Jesus himself taught us – and he started by encouraging us to call God 'Our Father'. For some people, that is easy – their own father was an ideal role model, a friend and always around for them. For an increasing number of people, the concept of a father is hard and remote – this sketch tries to acknowledge that this is now commonplace in the church as much as everywhere else.*

**How you might use it . . .**

There are four characters: someone whose father was everything they felt a father should be; someone who never knew their father, only their mother; someone who was physically abused by their father; and someone whose relationship with their father was never as good as it seemed to those around. This sketch is best performed with the four people separated as far as possible from each other, creating their own 'space' for their own viewpoint. If an OHP is available, the outline of a man could be projected with the words 'Our Father?' across the figure.

1      *(Prayerfully)* Our Father in heaven.

2      *(Sharp)* He's not my Father.

3      *(Quiet)* Or mine.

4      *(Quiet)* Whose Father is he then?

1      *(Confidently)* My father was a good man.

2      *(Shrugs)* I never knew mine.

3      *(Quiet)* I don't like to talk about mine.

4      *(Bitter)* Everyone thought my father was great – except me.

1      *(Adoringly)* My father talked to me, took me places, told me how much he loved me.

3      *(Deliberately)* My father beat me because I didn't win the school prize.

4    (Slowly) My father was always there but somehow he wasn't.

2    (Shrugs) My father? He could have been an astronaut or he could have been a road sweeper – I don't know and I don't care.

1    (Warm) Whenever I think of my father, I feel all warm and loving inside.

4    (Slowly) Whenever I think of my father, I want to know who he really was.

3    (Getting upset) Whenever I think of my father, I want to know 'Why?'

2    (Resigned) I couldn't care less about who my father was.

4    (Frowning – slowly) He's not a bad man – just distant and hard to understand.

3    (Questioning, getting angry) I must have done something to make him hate me all of those years.

1    (Dramatic) My father is my hero.

2    (Unsure) He may be good, he may be bad – all I know is that he has never been there.

1    (Worshipfully) We all looked up to him, my mother adored him.

3    (Angry) We were all scared of him – we never knew what he was going to do or who he was going to hit next.

4    (Thoughtfully) Sometimes it was a bit like having a stranger in the house – I've spent my whole life trying to reach him, hoping he'd love me.

2    (Thoughtfully) My mother is the only parent I have – she has always loved and cared for me and she's always been there.

1    (Confidently) God as my father? No problem – I look at my father and I can see God.

3    (Lost) God as my father? Vindictive, abusive and violent? Can a God like that really exist?

**4** *(Questioning)* God as my father? Distant and hard to find – always beyond my reach?

**2** *(Shrugs)* God as my father? What is a father?

**1** *(Warmly)* What *is* a father? A father to me is . . . *(Trails off into thought)*

**3** *(Bitterly)* What *is* a father? A father to me is . . . *(Trails off into thought)*

**4** *(Uncertainly and slowly)* What *is* a father?

### Questions you might like to think about . . .

- What are the attributes of a perfect parent? Can we see those in God – and, if so, where in the Bible do we see them?
- In Matthew 23:37 Jesus talked of God as being like a mother hen. Has God got male and female characteristics? Why, then, did Jesus call God 'Father'?
- List the parables where God is portrayed as a father. What do they tell us about God as our Father?

# Gimme, gimme, gimme, gimme

*'Give us this day our daily bread' – but what are we really asking for? Bread that is food, bread that is money . . . what is bread?*

**How you might use it . . .**

This could be read into one microphone by two people facing each other. A rap beat in the background would help the rhythm – this could either be prerecorded or using a keyboard rhythm key but the use of 'live' tom-toms allows for pauses as required.

**A**    Gimme.

**B**    Gimme.

**A**    Gimme.

**B**    Gimme.

**A**    Gimme what?

**B**    Gimme everything.

**A**    Gimme all I want.

**B**    Gimme bread.

**A**    Bread?

**B**    Bread, dough, dosh – I can buy what I want, or steal the rest.

**A**    The love of money is the root of all evil.

**B**    Rubbish – it's the freedom to buy what you want.

**A**    With freedom comes responsibility.

**B**   Who needs responsibility – enjoy it, that's what I say.

*(Pause)*

**A**   Gimme.

**B**   Gimme.

**A**   Gimme.

**B**   Gimme.

**A**   Gimme what?

**B**   Gimme everything.

**A**   Gimme all I need.

**B**   Gimme bread.

**A**   Bread?

**B**   Bread – what I need to live on.

**A**   Man shall not live by bread alone

**B**   but every word that proceeds from the mouth of God.

**A**   Fine – I'll eat God's words and starve to death.

**B**   Your Father in heaven only gives good things to his children.

**A**   Then give me what I need to survive.

*(Pause)*

**B**   Gimme.

**A**   Gimme.

**B**   Gimme.

**A**   Gimme.

**B** Gimme what?

**A** Gimme everything.

**B** Gimme all I need to live.

**A** Gimme bread.

**B** Bread?

**A** Give us this day our daily bread

  *(Pause)*

**B** in the middle of a world that says

**A** gimme

**B** gimme

**A** gimme

**B** gimme.

**A** Give us this day what we need:

**B** love

**A** the warmth of relationships

**B** shelter

**A** care

**B** health

**A** water to drink

**B** food to eat

**A** bread

**B** and wine.

**A**     This is my body

**B**     this is my blood.

**A**     Give us this day our daily bread.

**B**     Give us Jesus.

**A**     Give us life.


**Questions you might like to think about . . .**

- Do we already have what we need as opposed to what we think we need?

- Jesus said, 'Man shall not live by bread alone.' But how can we live without 'bread'?

- How do those with nothing understand 'Give us this day our daily bread'? What does it mean for them, when nothing arrives on their plate?

# Sorry, Lord

*Many church services include a prayer of confession, saying 'sorry' to God for the things we wish we hadn't done or the things we should have done. There is often the temptation to rush through this prayer without understanding something of the importance of saying 'sorry' – and really meaning it. This sketch consists of someone praying such a prayer and not expecting it to be answered.*

**How you might use it . . .**

It is best performed with 'God' as a disembodied voice by using a radio microphone or one with a long lead, putting 'God' in another room – but it is very important that God can hear the prayer!

**Man**     Lord God.

**God**     Not everyone who calls me Lord will enter the kingdom of heaven . . .

**Man**     Almighty God.

**God**     . . . but those who do my will.

**Man**     We have sinned against you . . .

**God**     Excuse me!

**Man**     and against our neighbour . . .

**God**     Hang on!

**Man**     through negligence, through weakness . . .

**God**     Wait!

**Man**     through our own deliberate fault . . .

**God**     STOP!!!

**Man**     *(Looks around)* uh . . . what's the matter?

**God**   What exactly are you trying to say?

**Man**   *(Thinks)* Sorry, I suppose.

**God**   Sorry?

**Man**   Yes . . . uh . . . sorry.

**God**   What for?

**Man**   Well, the things I've done wrong, I suppose.

**God**   Like . . . ?

**Man**   Er, like getting annoyed with the wife . . . again, and using words that the vicar would *not* like to hear and saying those things last week about that woman in the *awful* hat in church, and not admitting to be undercharged in the pub on Friday and . . .

**God**   Yes, yes, all right . . . but *why* are you sorry?

**Man**   Because I am.

**God**   Yes, but *why*? *(Pause)* Because your wife burst into tears and made you feel guilty? Because the woman in church heard your comment and glared? Because someone saw you pocket the change and said he didn't think Christians did that sort of thing? *Why?*

**Man**   *(Slowly)* I suppose because I chose to say and do these things.

**God**   You wanted to do them.

**Man**   Yes.

**God**   And *now* you're sorry.

**Man**   Yes.

**God**   WHY?

**Man**   Because I made the wrong choice? Because the decisions hurt you? Because they only go to show that I do what I want?

**God**   All of them.

**Man**   So what can I do about it?

**God**   Be sure you know why you're sorry – and *then* say it.

**Man**   *(Pause)* Sorry. *(Thinks)* But why is it that even when I say sorry, I still do them again, like that incident in the pub . . .

**God**   What incident?

**Man**   The one we were just talking about.

**God**   I don't remember it.

**Man**   You know, the one about not admitting getting too much change, along with the other things about hats, my wife and bad language in front of the vicar . . .

**God**   As I said, I don't remember it.

**Man**   You *must* do!!

**God**   I don't.

**Man**   How can you forget – you're supposed to be omnisci–, omnis-scie–, you're supposed to know everything.

**God**   I do – but someone made me forget.

**Man**   What do you mean, someone?

**God**   Him.

**Man**   *(Dawning)* Oh . . . him! So when he died . . .

**God**   . . . he sorted it out . . . and made me forget.

**Man**   All of it?

**God** All of it – every little bit of it – sorted. And when he died, he took with him all those things you say you did.
It wasn't easy. It cost him pain . . .
Bosnia, Northern Ireland, Rwanda, Dunblane,
thousands of years of sin and hatred,
all rolled into one man's pain . . .

**Man** *(In wonder)* . . . and *all* of it was taken away?

**God** *Completely.* As far as the east is from the west.

**Man** In other words, all that I've done wrong . . . is gone – as if it had never happened.

**God** What were Jesus' final words on the cross?

**Man** 'It is finished.'

**God** The job was finished – completely. How do you finish your prayer of saying 'sorry'?

**Man** Grant that we may serve you in newness of life, to the glory of your name. Amen.

**God** Newness of life – a fresh start. To whose glory?

**Man** Yours, not mine.

**God** Amen.

**Man** Amen.

**Questions you might like to think about . . .**

- When we say, 'Forgive us as we forgive those who sin against us', what are the effects when we don't forgive others?

- Can we forgive people who aren't sorry?

- What happens when we pray for forgiveness and then don't allow ourselves to be forgiven?

- Is it possible for us to 'forgive and forget'? Does God do it?

# There's danger out there!

*The idea that somehow we are all involved in a spiritual battle is one that is quite unnerving for many Christians, and most of us hope that 'lead us not into temptation' and 'deliver us from evil' are sufficient prayers to mean that we will not be involved at the forefront of the battle. This sketch aims to encourage Christians to accept that we have no choice but to be involved in the spiritual battle of the world in which we live – and keeping our ears, eyes and heart fixed on the commander will bring us through.*

**How you might use it . . .**

The officer is laid back, efficient and confident of the eventual outcome whereas the soldier is enthusiastic but naive – this sketch is a golden opportunity for overacting! Some uniforms would add to the effect and the sketch could begin with a dramatic entry as the soldier marches in shouting, 'Left, right, left right . . . about turn . . . present arms . . .' and any other suitable phrases.

| | |
|---|---|
| **Officer** | Name, rank and number! |
| **Soldier** | Foot Soldier Second Class Woodhurst, 315454, reporting for duty, saaah! |
| **Officer** | OK, Woodhurst . . . it's the big push . . . how do you feel? |
| **Soldier** | Itching to get at 'em, saaah! |
| **Officer** | All right, all right, settle down, settle down Woodhurst . . . this is serious. |
| **Soldier** | *(Calmed down)* Serious, sir? |
| **Officer** | Yes, serious . . . people are going to get hurt out there! |
| **Soldier** | Hurt, sir? |
| **Officer** | Yes, hurt, Woodhurst . . . and . . . you've got to get out there and do your bit. |

**Soldier**     Well, I'll be all right, sir, my mum always said I lived a charmed life – I'll be back here tonight, right as rain, sir!

**Officer**     I think you may be taking this all a little lightly, Woodhurst.

**Soldier**     Oh no, sir – don't know the meaning of the word 'danger', sir!

**Officer**     I don't think you realise just how much danger there is out there.

**Soldier**     I've read the books, sir, and seen the films . . . *The Dirty Dozen, Ice Station Zebra, Where Eagles Dare* . . .

**Officer**     Woodhurst, those are just stories . . . this is reality!

**Soldier**     Reality, sir?

**Officer**     Yes, reality – where people do get hurt, where the hero can be killed – and that includes you, Woodhurst.

**Soldier**     *(Pauses, and then, very fearfully)* Do you think you could get by without me today, sir?

**Officer**     No, Woodhurst, we can't – you already have tasks assigned to you, jobs that only you have been trained for and you are an essential part of the team.

**Soldier**     But sir, what if a sniper picks me off as I leave here . . . what if I forget all that I've learned in training . . . what if I walk straight into an ambush . . . what if . . . sir, I'd like to resign right now.

**Officer**     Sorry, Woodhurst, too late, the enemy already knows who you are and if you walk out of here, he'll be after you.

**Soldier**     But I'm scared, sir.

**Officer**     Yes . . . none of us knows what is lying ahead of us. But don't you think I'm going to go out there with you? Don't you think the General has officer plan for today? Don't you think you have a place in that plan?

**Soldier**     So I don't have anything to worry about?

**Officer**   Woodhurst . . . what is the safest thing you can do today?

**Soldier**   Follow orders, sir.

**Officer**   And what happens later on, in the confusion of battle, when people have got separated from their units?

**Soldier**   Use the radio to make sure we don't lose touch, sir.

**Officer**   Why?

**Soldier**   So that we can get further orders, sir.

**Officer**   So what is the most important thing for you to do today?

**Soldier**   Keep in touch with HQ, sir.
Keep close to the commander, you, sir.
Keep following orders so that I won't be tempted to stray from the battle plan.
Keep listening for your voice and trusting you not to lead me into danger, sir.

**Officer**   Give me two words that sum it up, Woodhurst.

**Soldier**   Trust and obey, sir, trust and obey.

**Officer**   You've got it Woodhurst – now go and do it: trust and obey.

### Questions you might like to think about . . .

- In what ways could life be described as a battle?
- Which are the times when we are in the front line?
- Is everyone called to be in the front line?
- What are the dangers of overemphasising the battle by interpreting everything that happens in terms of warfare or underemphasising it by denying its existence?
- What kinds of soldiers are there? Which roles in church life could they be likened to?

# The point of life

*This sketch is intended to pose questions – not answer them. Many Christians do not take the wider view of life which goes beyond questions of their own salvation – this aims to get people thinking about the deepest questions about who we are and why we are here.*

## How you might use it . . .

The two characters in this sketch could possibly arrive from opposite ends of the room, one whistling, one lost in thought, until they casually meet at the front. There could then be a pause whilst they look around, clearly lost in thought. Aspects of the sketch (e.g. the names, the situation in which it is performed and other characters referred to in the sketch) can easily be amended to make it relevant to the audience.

**David**   Well, here we are.

**Paul**   He we are, indeed.

*(Pause)*

**David**   There's a question – why are we here?

**Paul**   Well, to fulfil the literary aspirations of our curate who thinks he's the Shakespeare of the church drama scene . . .

**David**   No . . . *Why* are we here?

**Paul**   Because it's the last one of the Lord's Prayer series and the vicar's keeping a register?

**David**   *No . . . Why are we here?* On this earth, living . . . being people? What is it all for?

**Paul**   I know someone who used to wonder whether it was all some kind of experiment, and he was the subject of it.

**David**   What, like we're all under a microscope – God's microscope?

**Paul**   Something like that, anyway.

*(Pause)*

**David**  So, anyway, why are we here?

**Paul**  Whenever I asked questions like that to my mum she always used to give a really deep philosophical answer.

**David**  Which was . . . ?

**Paul**  Because '*y*' has got a long tail.

**David**  Well, thank you very much Paul's mum . . . we're all here because '*y*' has got a long tail. That's *really* helpful.

*(Pause)*

**David**  So why *are* we here?

**Paul**  I've given you enough answers.

**David**  All you've given me are silly answers . . . I want to know the truth.

**Paul**  Aaah . . . truth, what *is* truth?

**David**  Oh, don't start again! All I want to know is whether there is a point to all of this: living, eating, breathing, marrying, having kids, getting old . . . dying?

**Paul**  Why do you want to know?

*(Pause)*

**David**  Either there is a point to all of this, or there isn't . . . right?

**Paul**  Right.

**David**  And if there isn't a point to all of this, then it's all a bit of a waste of time and we're just doing all of these things to make sure that there are more people after us – we're just making sure the pointlessness of it all continues.

**Paul**    Yeeees?

**David**    But if there is a point to all of this, then it means there must be someone in charge and if so, I think he, she or it must have some idea what the purpose of all of this is.

**Paul**    So . . . ?

**David**    I want to know what that purpose is!

**Paul**    Meaning . . . ?

**David**    *Why are we here!*

## Questions you might like to think about . . .

- So what *is* the point of life? Is there a point to each individual life or is it to contribute to the whole?
- Is there a point in our lives which defines our own life, for example, a moment where we 'peak'?
- When we look back over our life, maybe as an older person, what would we like to see?
- Do you think it might be possible to see the purpose being worked out throughout our lives?

# WE ARE . . .

# Salt 'n' light

*This sketch is based on the passage in Matthew 5:13-16, where Jesus tells his disciples that they are the salt of the earth and they are light to the world. The two have been lumped together so often that the differences between them are sometimes forgotten. This sketch aims to separate the two and help us realise that we need to be both of them.*

**How you might use it . . .**

This is best performed with the two readers separated by a reasonable distance, emphasising the differences between them. Two overhead projectors with slides of a light and a salt shaker could be turned on as the actors read the lines 'I am light/I am salt'. Alternatively, suitable props could be put on a small table in front of them or between them.

**Light**      You can't see me.

  **Salt**      You can see me.

**Light**      You can see what I show you.

  **Salt**      You can taste me.

**Light**      I can show you the world.

  **Salt**      I can make things taste good.

**Light**      I can show you the tiniest speck.

  **Salt**      I can keep things fresh.

**Light**      I am light.

  **Salt**      I am salt.

**Light**      Light shows the path ahead.

  **Salt**      Salt cleanses.

**Light**      Light shows the things which need attention.

**Salt**      Salt is essential to life.

**Light**      Life without light would be dark and meaningless.

**Salt**      Life without salt would be dull and tasteless.

**Light**      We need both light

**Salt**      and salt.

**Light**      Salt

**Salt**      and light.

**Light**      One

**Salt**      without the other

**Light**      means tasting something you cannot see

**Salt**      or seeing something you cannot taste.

**Light**      We need both.

**Salt**      We need both.

**Light**      Jesus said, 'You are the light of the world.'

**Salt**      Jesus said, 'You are the salt of the earth.'

**Light**      Give the world my light – show it the things that are hidden and the path ahead.

**Salt**      Give the world my salt – keep it fresh to give it taste.

**Light**      You will know when my work is done.

**Salt**      You will know when my work is done.

**Questions you might like to think about . . .**

Look up the passage in Matthew 5:13-16.

- What are the effects of lamp shades, mirrors, lenses . . . ?
- What are the lamps, mirrors and lenses that are light to the world?

John 1:9 – 'The true light that gives light to every man was coming into the world.'

- How does the light of man-made bulbs differ?
- How can we intensify the true light?
- Salt is sharp to the taste when it is on its own. How can we liken that to being salt in the world?
- Should we look for things to soften the taste/the effect?

# The branch line

*When Jesus talked of his followers as the branches in John 15:5, he was thinking of the way that branches need the main trunk of the vine or tree to exist – they receive their nourishment from it and without it they would certainly die. This sketch talks about a branch line of a railway in similar terms.*

## How you might use it . . .

The 'bing-bong' and announcement at the start are best done using a prerecorded message played over a church PA system – but can be done to comic effect by the actors themselves. Suitable props such as an official-looking cap, a whistle and a flag for the Guard, and a suit and briefcase (or even a bowler hat) for the Passenger would add to the effect of this sketch. The increased exasperation of the traveller faced with the rather miserable story of the Guard can be built up as the sketch progresses so that each new revelation about the state of the railway seems more ridiculous than the last.

*'Bing-bong'*

**Guard**  *(Muffled sound)* The train arriving at Platform 1 is the 18:32 express to Self-fulfilment calling at all stops beyond Selflessness and Caring. Due to unforeseen circumstances the connection with Greater Being will be made via a coach journey from Little Hope. Thank you for travelling with Independent Railways.

*'Bing-bong'*

**Passenger**  Um . . . excuse me.

**Guard**  What?

**Passenger**  I seem to be lost and I was wondering if you could help me?

**Guard**  How?

**Passenger**  Well, I'm trying to get to Greater Being and I was . . .

**Guard**    Don't you lot ever listen to announcements? There is no connection to Greater Being from here except using the coach connection at Little Hope.

**Passenger**    But I've always been told that you could get to Greater Being from anywhere on this line.

**Guard**    Aah . . . aaah! You *used* to be able to get there on this line and then it all got privatised, didn't it?

**Passenger**    But isn't this a branch line?

**Guard**    *(Morosely)* It used to be.

**Passenger**    But it isn't any more?

**Guard**    No – they pulled up the line where it connected to the main line because the new owners wouldn't pay the bill. But, look on the bright side: We've got some great express services and they have a great time going up and down this track.

**Passenger**    Um . . . how long is this branch line?

**Guard**    Now – there's a question! Me and Sid – he's the station master – we're always arguing about this. He reckons it's two miles and I reckon it's two and a quarter.

**Passenger**    So let me get this straight. You run Inter City 125s along a track two miles long . . .

**Guard**    Two and a quarter . . .

**Passenger**    Whatever . . . and you have no connection with the main line.

**Guard**    That's about it . . . well, for the moment.

**Passenger**    For the moment?

**Guard**    It doesn't look as though we will survive as a going concern.

**Passenger**    I'm not surprised. Look – why don't you try and join up with the main line?

**Guard**    Well, it means paying the bill and the people who own this track don't want to.

**Passenger**    How much *is* the bill?

**Guard**    Oh – it's nothing – zippo, zilch, freebie.

**Passenger**    Hang on a moment! Are you trying to tell me that they won't pay a bill that doesn't exist?

**Guard**    That's not the point – it's the principle that counts.

**Passenger**    What on earth are you talking about?

**Guard**    If we pay the bill . . .

**Passenger**    . . . that's for nothing.

**Guard**    All right, that's for nothing, then we have to let them run their trains on our branch line.

**Passenger**    But then you can run your trains on the main line, which is where they're meant to be!

**Guard**    That's true – but then we can't control them, can we? Who knows where the main-line owner might send them, eh? North of Scotland, Penzance . . . anywhere!

**Passenger**    But that's what is meant to happen to them. And if you join up to the main line you might get more passengers, mightn't you?

**Guard**    Passengers?

**Passenger**    Yes, passengers, people – people who sit on trains . . . and pay for the privilege.

**Guard**    Oh . . . I remember passengers.

**Passenger**    You mean you don't have passengers?

**Guard**  Not since privatisation – nasty, smelly, grubby things sitting on our nice clean seats, making it all dirty. No – that all stopped when we went out on our own.

**Passenger**  *(Sighs)* What's the point?

**Guard**  What's what point?

**Passenger**  What's the point of having a branch line with all the wrong trains on it, no passengers, and going absolutely nowhere (except broke) because you don't want to lose control of your useless business?

**Guard**  Now you come to think of it, it does seem a little silly. *(Cheering up)* Never mind, there's always tomorrow. *(Saddens)* Except, I don't think there will be a tomorrow because I think we'll have to close down; and everything, trains, track, rolling-stock . . . me . . . all on the scrap heap – worthless.

**Passenger**  Well, I still want to get to Greater Being . . . how far is it to the main-line station?

**Guard**  The other end of the platform.

**Passenger**  The other end of the platform?

**Guard**  It only takes a couple of feet of track to lose a branch line.

**Passenger**  You coming with me? A couple of feet isn't far to go!

**Guard**  Sorry – hopeless or not, I'm stuck here – two feet is just too far to go. *(Calls)* Mind the doors!

*(Passenger shrugs and walks away)*

**Questions you might like to think about . . .**

Look up the passage in Matthew 5:13-16.

- Being connected to the vine/trunk means a lot of things.
- How might we interpret different aspects of the picture? For example:
  sap, the life-blood of trees?
  leaves that change colour and fall each autumn?
  roots that give strength?
- What is the purpose of the fruit of a vine?
- What is the purpose of the Fruit of the Spirit? (Galatians 5:22-23)
- What might different branches of the vine represent?
- How do they relate to each other – simply because they both link to the main body/trunk, or is there more?

# The Body of Christ

*In 1 Corinthians 12:12, Paul discusses various aspects of the body of Christ but leaves us to work out just which bits refer to which people in the Church – this sketch suggests possible labels for some but hopefully shows that all of us, insignificant or not, have a part to play and are important to the body as a whole.*

## How you might use it . . .

A face-to-face conversation (as used by Mel Smith and Griff Rhys-Jones) could add to this sketch, especially if the two actors can face each other across a table lit only by two anglepoise lamps. A possible ending would be to turn the lights off after the last line.

**David**   So *we* are the Body of Christ.

**Paul**   Yep.

**David**   You don't look much like him.

**Paul**   Neither do you.

**David**   I mean – if you and I are supposed to look like the body of Christ – neither of us look much like the windows in our church . . .

**Paul**   Um . . . I don't think that's what it means.

**David**   Well, what does it mean then?

**Paul**   It means that all the Christians in the world sort of make up the whole Body of Christ on earth.

**David**   And what, if I may be so bold to ask, does all of that gobbledygook mean?

**Paul**   Well, just before he went back to heaven, Jesus told all his mates that they were to carry on his work and that between them they had all the gifts and all the talents that he had, and so they were, in one sense, 'him'.

**David** *(Not really understanding)* Uuuuh-huh.

**Paul** So the Church is, by with or from, as it were, in a manner of speaking, the Body of Christ on earth because we are the successors of Jesus' mates.

**David** What, all of us – including that lot out there, my Auntie Elsie in Dundee and all the people in Poland, Venezuela, Outer Mongolia, France . . . ?

**Paul** Yes, yes, *all* of us – but we're all different bits of the Body.

**David** Euuch! What, like one person's a left toenail and another's an elbow?

**Paul** Something like that.

*(They pause, thinking)*

**David** I reckon I know who the hands are.

**Paul** Go on . . .

**David** The Pope and the Archbishop of Canterbury.

**Paul** Why?

**David** Well, the press are always saying, 'On the one hand, the Pope says this and on the other the Archbishop says that'.

**Paul** I see.

**David** Seriously though, they could be the hands.

**Paul** Why?

**David** Well, your hands are opposite to each other, aren't they?

**Paul** And?

**David** Well, Pope-y and Arch-y are in some ways very different but they need each other, just like we need both hands when there's a difficult job to do. The hands work together – just like your legs work together and all the other bits of the body have to work together.

**Paul** So, all the different bits of the body

**David** have to work together to make it function. *(Proud)* Good, eh?

*(They pause again, thinking)*

**Paul** So which bits of the body are there?

**David** The ears.

**Paul** That must be the people who are good at hearing God speak.

**David** The mouth.

**Paul** The ones who tell people about Jesus.

**David** The feet.

**Paul** The ones who work in other countries or in difficult places for God.

**David** The armpits.

**Paul** The armpits?

**David** Well, if we can say who all the other bits are, we must be able to say who the armpits are.

*(They pause again, thinking)*

**Paul** The armpits get smelly and sweaty when the body does a lot of work.

**David** Like the people who put the chairs and tables away after meetings. *(Pause, thinking)* Bet they never thought of themselves as armpits.

*(Pause)*

**Paul**   So which bit of the body are you, then?

**David**   *(Thinks hard)* Um.

**Paul**   Well, it certainly isn't the brain.

**David**   Thank you.

**Paul**   Probably some insignificant little bit somewhere near the left ankle.

**David**   Less of the insignificant little bit, thank you. It says that the body needs all of its bits – even the bits that don't look very nice. So we know where you fit in.

   *(Pause)*

**Paul**   Interesting though, isn't it?

**David**   Mmmm.

**Paul**   Question – who's the heart?

**David**   Good question.

**Paul**   The heart pumps blood around the body.

**David**   It's the source of all it's life and energy.

**Paul**   So . . . who's the heart?

**David**   Have to think about that one – it's nobody on this earth I can think of.

   *(They exit, thinking)*

**Questions you might like to think about . . .**

Look up the passage in 1 Corinthians 12:12-31.

- So, who is the heart?
- What about the head? (Look at Colossians 2:19)
- The body functions due to a host of unseen activity – what does that say to us?
- What are the factors that keep a body in good condition?
- What are the similar factors that keep the Body of Christ in good condition?
- Look at John 2:21; 1 Corinthians 6:19 and 1 Peter 2:5. How do these images of buildings relate to the image of the Church as the Body of Christ?

# BITS 'N' BOBS
# ALONG THE WAY

# The story of the fantastic father

## (The prodigal son)

*This is a straight-forward telling of the story of the prodigal son. Thanks to Mike Chadwick for the original idea.*

**How you might use it . . .**

This involves a little preparation but visually it is fun and fast and can be developed depending on the venue. Where no pulpit is available, some form of staging or chairs could provide a suitable lookout. The story is set in two parts to emphasise the passing of time and a song could be sung between them on the subject of forgiveness. The song used in the sketch should be one with which most people are familiar (preferably a song which has become synonymous with parties).

Characters: Narrator, Father, Son, Girls (two or three).

The Narrator can be seen, standing close to the action and the actors can (if they wish) bring him into the action, for example, dancing with him, nodding 'hello' to him, etc. The Father is a well-to-do business man, preferably in pinstripe three-piece suit, whereas the Son is in the midst of classic teenage rebellion and can be dressed in the most extreme way possible! The Girls, too, can wear the current club outfit!

### Part 1. The Departure

**Narrator**     A big house, a big estate, somewhere . . .

*(Enter Son from one side – looking for his dad)*

**Son**     Dad . . . Dad . . . *Daaad*!

*(Father enters from other side)*

**Father**     Yes, my son?

**Son**  (*Casually*) Hello Dad! Hiya!  Heeello!

**Father**  Yes, hello . . . *[Name]*

**Son**  Hello my dear, wonderful Father.

**Father**  What do you want?

**Son**  Oh, uh . . . nothing! Nothing at all!

**Father**  Come on, out with it, what do you want?

**Son**  Well . . . you know when you die . . .

**Father**  Yeees?

**Son**  Well, you know me and my brother are going to get all you own – the company, the house, the cars and all your lovely dosh?

**Father**  Yeees?

**Son**  Can I have my bit now?

**Father**  *What???*

**Son**  Can I have it now – you know, enjoy it . . . now.

**Father**  Why now?

**Son**  Well – so as I can enjoy it while I'm young and free and full of fun!

**Father**  (*Thinks*) Well, I suppose if that's what you want – I'll arrange it for you.

**Son**  Thanks Dad . . . I won't forget it.

(*They both exit*)

**Narrator**  Some time later . . .

*(Son crosses 'stage' with massive suitcase, dropping money on the way)*

**Narrator**  Some time even later . . .

*(Enter Father)*

**Father**  I wonder how *[Name]* is getting on?

*(Exit)*

**Narrator**  Well – let's see . . .

*(Music – The latest pop chart hit or similar is heard. Balloons are thrown on to 'stage' with streamers. Son crosses stage with a Girl on each arm, talking to them and imaginary people all around)*

**Son**  Hi . . . Hi . . . Hi!! How are you . . . have a drink. No, I insist – let me buy it for you!
 *(To Girls)* You want a new car? – no problem! Hi . . . Hello!

**Narrator**  Some time later . . .

*(Father wanders across 'stage', obviously worried)*

**Father**  I wonder how *[Name]* is getting on – I haven't heard from him for so long.

*(Exit)*

**Narrator**  Well . . .

*(Music – The same music is heard but played slower. Fewer balloons with fewer streamers. Son crosses stage with one Girl on his arm, talking to her)*

**Son**  I don't know where everyone is tonight. Well, you and I can enjoy this evening. Have a drink! Look – I promised you I'd buy a car and I will. It's just that cash is running a bit low.

**Narrator**  Back at home . . .

*(Father wanders across 'stage', very worried)*

**Father**  [Name] hasn't phoned for ages. What can be going on?

*(Exit)*

*(Music – same music – slowly at first, then grinds to a halt. One balloon bounces on to 'stage' with one streamer. Son wanders on to stage alone, looking dishevelled)*

**Son**  I don't know what's going on! I had lots of friends when I had lots of money. Now I haven't got either. I haven't got a job. I can't afford to rent somewhere to live and I can't even afford to eat.

I've been rummaging in the bins around the back of Sainsbury's but there hasn't been much there.

I can't go home, I've blown all of Dad's money – he isn't going to want to see me. What can I do? What can I do? *(He wanders off, alone)*

## Part 2. The Return

**Narrator**  [Name] has been gone a long time – and his father is desperate for news.

*(Father goes into pulpit, obviously looking for his son)*

**Narrator**  Months have passed. The son's father has phoned hundreds of people and sent out detectives looking for him.

Apart from hearing stories of his son spending all of the money, the father doesn't know where his son is.

*(Son appears at the back of church – in a terrible state. The father doesn't see him, but carries on looking. The son wanders forward, talking to himself)*

**Son**  There's nothing else I can do. I've no one else to turn to. Maybe Dad will give me a job in the factory. I'll do anything – anything at all.

I'll just have to come clean and say, 'Dad – I've blown it all and I've nothing left. All that you gave me – it's gone. I'm sorry – I am really sorry. Look, is there any chance,

any chance at all that I can come and work for you?'
*(Father spots him and rushes down out of the pulpit, shouting)*

**Father**  *(Calling his son's name repeatedly)* It's you!!!

*(Son falls on his knees in front of father who is now at front of church)*

**Son**  Dad – look, I've blown it all and I've nothing left. I'm sorry, I am really sorry. Look, is there any chance, any chance at all that I can come and work for you?

**Father**  *[Name]* it is wonderful to see you! Come in, we've got to have a party!

**Son**  But I can't be your son any more – I've spent all that you gave me.

**Father**  You are still my son – you didn't stop being my son.

*(Father and son turn to face audience)*

**Father**  This is my son. Just like everyone of you he has made mistakes.

He has probably made more than any of you – but he is still my son. And I love him and nothing can change that. I just love him and care about him. Come on, son.

*(Father and son turn and go 'into the house')*

**Narrator**  Jesus said that God is like the father. It doesn't matter how much we have done wrong, God will always forgive us and welcome us back.

God loves us and cares for us, his children, and nothing will ever change that.

**Questions you might like to think about . . .**

Look up the story in Luke 15:11-32.

- Are we all prodigal children?
- Is it necessary to reach the bottom before we understand our need of God?
- Who does the older brother in this story relate to?
- Put yourself in the shoes of the father and those of the sons: why did they react the way they did?

The questions relating to 'Whose Father?' may also be relevant.

# Who's the greatest?

## (The Transfiguration)

*Two children/young people are arguing about the best pop group ever and the adults join in, initially trying to stop the argument. Eventually they see the feet of clay in all man-made gods. This is a useful introduction to the story of the Transfiguration but could be used with other stories.*

**How you might use it . . .**

This sketch could be used in a variety of settings, in a school setting or round a table at home. The names of the contemporary bands will need to be updated – the young actors may well offer their own suggestions, and the argument may become real! The disembodied voice could be provided by someone in another room, using a radio microphone or a microphone with a long lead, but make sure they can hear enough to know when their cue is.

*(Child A and Child B enter)*

**Child A**    Look, *N1\** are streets ahead of *N2*!

**Child B**    Rubbish – *N2* have had more hits – they're the greatest ever!

**Child A**    But they've not been around very long, have they? They'll break up before long.

**Child B**    But they're selling more than *N1*.

*(Discussion gets heated)*

**Child A**    *N1* are the best band ever.

**Child B**    No – *N2* are.

**Child A**    *N1*!

* *N1* and *N2*: use the names of current chart-topping boy/girl pop groups

**Child B**   *N2!*

*(Enter Adult A)*

**Adult A**   Hey – what are you two arguing about?

**Child A**   I think *N1* are the best group ever.

**Child B**   No they're not – *N2* are!

*(They start arguing again)*

**Adult A**   OK, OK, stop! Does it matter?

**Child B**   We just want to know; who is the best?

**Adult A**   Well – I suppose if it comes down to it – neither of them are. The best band ever were the Beatles.

**Child B**   The who?

**Adult A**   No, the Beatles.

*(Adult B enters)*

**Adult B**   What's the discussion about?

**Adult A**   Just deciding who the greatest band ever were – I was just telling them it was the Beatles.

**Child A**   *N1!*

**Child B**   *N2!*

**Adult B**   Actually, it was none of them – everyone knows that Eric Clapton is the greatest.

**Child A & B**   Who?

**Adult B**   No, Eric Clapton.

**Adult A**   I've done that one already.

**Adult B**    People used to write on the walls, 'Clapton is God'.

**Child A**    Well, I reckon that *N1* are gods.

**Child B**    And *N2*.

**Adult A**    People used to think the Beatles were gods.

**Child A**    What happened?

**Adult A**    They found out that they were only people. They got messed up with all sorts of stuff and we soon realised that even if they were the best band ever they were still people like us.

**Adult B**    Same with Clapton – pretty messed-up life.

**Child A**    Well, that won't happen with *N1*.

**Child B**    Or *N2*.

**Adult A**    Don't you think they are people like us?

**Child A**    I suppose so.

**Adult B**    Don't you think they do things wrong?

**Child B**    I suppose they must do.

**Child A**    Doesn't everyone?

**Adult A**    Every one of us does things wrong. Anyone who claims to be God – sooner or later we'll see them as they really are.

**Adult B**    Yes – we'll see them as they really are:

*(They all turn and face the congregation as a voice is heard)*

**Voice**    Jesus took Peter and James with him, and led them up a high mountain. Suddenly his appearance changed and they saw him for who he really was. His face shone like the sun, and his clothes became as white as the light. Then Moses and Elijah, two great men of the Old Testament, appeared, talking with

Jesus. Peter said, 'Lord, it is brilliant that we are here. If you like, I will put up three shelters – one for you, one for Moses and one for Elijah.'

Just as he was speaking, a bright cloud enveloped them, and a voice from the cloud said, 'This is my Son, whom I love; I am well pleased with him. Listen to him!'

### Questions you might like to think about . . .

Look up the story in Matthew 16:1-9; Mark 9:2-13; Luke 9:28-36.

- When Jesus was changed, what were the disciples actually seeing?
- Why did Peter say what he did? What would you have said?
- Why do we want to place value on people such as pop stars?
- Would you like to be seen as you really are? By others? By God? Why? Why not?

# Sensible Cyril and Twittish Trevor

## (The wise and foolish builders)

*The message of the Gospel is one that involves taking risks; after all, isn't that what faith is all about? In this sketch it is Cyril who appears at first to be the wise builder, but in actual fact Trevor emerges as the sensible one – the one who knew that although he was a bit of a twit, his heart was firmly in the right place.*

**How you might use it . . .**

This sketch can be developed visually as far as the imagination and available props will allow! Whilst it could be used simply as a reading, the use of two other people to mime the characters allows for overacting and clowning on a grand scale. Clothes that emphasise the characters (including a set of plastic 'buckteeth' for Trevor) add to the comparisons between the characters. Some props are suggested below, but much, much more can be done locally to add to what is suggested here. The gnome, however, is compulsory!

*(Cyril and Trevor stand with their backs to the audience, some distance from narrators A and B. Cyril turns to face the audience and reacts to the descriptions of him with a smug expression.)*

**A**     Cyril was sensible.

**B**     Cyril was born sensible.

**A**     Cyril grew up sensible.

**B**     Cyril was a sensible man.

*(Cyril stands still. Trevor turns to face the audience and reacts to the descriptions of him with gooning and a 'dim' expression.)*

**A**     Trevor was a twit.

**B**   Trevor was born a twit.

**A**   Trevor grew up a twit.

**B**   Trevor was a man who knew he was a twit.

*(Trevor stands still. Whilst the description is read, Cyril holds up a briefcase, pats it, opens it, looks inside and nods knowingly at the papers inside.)*

**A**   Cyril was careful.

**B**   Cyril knew the value of things.

**A**   Cyril knew not to spend too much.

**B**   Not to go on expensive holidays abroad.

**A**   Not to buy flash cars.

**B**   Not to invest in one thing – but to spread it around.

**A**   Cyril's second name was Prudence.

*(Cyril looks up from his briefcase, concerned)*

**B**   But only to his close friends.

*(Cyril looks relieved)*

**A**   And there weren't too many of them

*(Cyril shakes his head)*

**B**   because Cyril wasn't the social sort.

*(Cyril puts briefcase down and stands still. Trevor grins a silly grin.)*

**A**   Trevor

**B**   on the other hand

**A**   may have been a bit of a twit

*(Trevor nods)*

**B**    but he enjoyed life.

*(Trevor nods even more and pulls out a party hat and blower)*

**A**    Money and possessions,

*(Trevor puts his hands in his pockets and pulls them out showing they are empty)*

**B**    he said,

**A**    are here today

**B**    and gone tomorrow.

*(Trevor blows blower and throws a streamer into the audience)*

**A**    Life,

**B**    he said,

**A**    is to be lived.

**B**    Trevor liked people

*(Trevor grins and opens his arms to the audience)*

**A**    more than things.

*(They both stand still)*

**B**    Cyril

**A**    and Trevor

**B**    bought houses.

**A**    Houses on a brand-new estate

**B**    somewhere posh.

*(Cyril holds up a model or cardboard cut-out of a large, posh house)*

**A**     Cyril bought a house at the top of the hill

**B**     because it was a sound investment.

*(Trevor holds up a model or cardboard-cut out of a small, insignificant house)*

**A**     Trevor bought a house at the bottom of the hill

**B**     because it was cheaper.

*(Trevor drops his house)*

**A**     And there they lived.

**B**     Cyril in his sensible, expensive house at the top of the hill

**A**     and Trevor in his cheaper house at the bottom of the hill –

**B**     with gnomes

*(Trevor picks up a gnome. Cyril looks disdainful)*

**A**     and an ornamental pond

*(Trevor picks up a plastic stork or some other garden feature)*

**B**     with a plastic stork in it

*(Trevor jigs around, with party hat, blower and arms full of garden things)*

**A**     which everyone had a good laugh about at the parties –

**B**     and there were many of them.

**A**     Until one day

**B**     Hurricane Gertrude came by

*(Someone off-stage throws several handfuls of leaves at Trevor and Cyril)*

**A**    along with the odd flood or two

**B**    and a rather nasty line in flying trees.

*(Cyril drops his house)*

**A**    Cyril's sensible house took a bit of a battering

**B**    and lost a few tiles.

*(Trevor drops everything – be careful with breakable gnomes!)*

**A**    But Trevor,

**B**    oh dear,

**A**    Trevor's house suddenly had an indoor swimming pool

**B**    which the architect certainly hadn't designed.

*(Cyril picks up briefcase and begins to search through papers, scattering some of them as he does so)*

**A**    Cyril called the insurance company

**B**    who didn't make a drama out of a crisis.

*(Trevor picks up his gnome and gently caresses it)*

**A**    Trevor called his mates

**B**    who had a good laugh

*(Trevor looks up and offers an inane grin)*

**A**    but mucked in

**B**    and dried him out.

*(Trevor puts his gnome down)*

*(Cyril and Trevor pick their houses up and look at them with concern)*

**A**    Then there was a recession

**B**    and house prices fell

**A**    and jobs were lost

*(Cyril and Trevor look up with shock and then look at each other)*

**B**    like Cyril's

**A**    and Trevor's

**B**    and Hurricane Gertrude seemed like a breeze.

**A**    Cyril

**B**    and Trevor.

*(Cyril picks up his house and looks at it, shaking his head)*

**A**    Sensible Cyril

**B**    in his sensible house

**A**    which he couldn't afford

**B**    with his sensible outlook

**A**    and not much else.

*(Trevor picks up his gnome by mistake and then picks up his house, holding it upside down)*

**B**    And Twittish Trevor

**A**    in his twittish house

*(Trevor puts the house down and opens his arms wide. Cyril fades into the background, still looking intently at his house)*

**B**    with his friends

**A**    oh yes, his friends

**B**    well, family, really.

**A**    He called them his family,

**B**    his family from the local church.

*(Trevor picks up his gnome, cuddles it and grins)*

**A**    Trevor was a twit

**B**    and he knew it

**A**    but he also knew

**B**    that God loves twits –

*(Trevor nods)*

**A**    and sensible people

*(Trevor points at Cyril with the hand not holding the gnome. Cyril looks up and then points at himself, surprised)*

**B**    and you

*(Trevor points at narrator A)*

**A**    and me –

*(Trevor points at narrator B)*

**B**    well, everyone really

*(Trevor points at the audience)*

**A**    but, especially those

**B**    who listen to the words of Jesus

**A**     and put them into practice.

*(Trevor nods with a very serious look on his face. He then gives the gnome a cuddle, grins, and walks off)*

### Questions you might like to think about . . .

Look up the story in Matthew 7:24-27; Luke 6:47-49.

- Trevor was a twit – but he knew it. Is it OK to remain a twit?
- In the eyes of the world, are Christians twits anyway?
- Why did the builders in the Bible story choose their respective plots?
- After the story in the Bible ended, what relationship existed between the wise and foolish man?
- Is this a story about decisions taken during our life – which can be changed? Or is it a story about the decision about our life as a whole?

# My new motor

## (Forgiveness)

*I have a cartoon by my desk which says, 'If love is the best policy, how come revenge feels so good?' Imagine the best possession you have, the one you saved up for, looked forward to . . . being ruined in a split second: that's when we learn the meaning of forgiveness.*

**How you might use it . . .**

There are a variety of settings in which this could be used, for example, in a pub with Phil leaning over the bar, in an office with Phil sitting at a table reading some papers, or in a house with Phil putting his feet up, reading the paper. The setting is not as important as finding someone who acts 'anger' as over the top as possible, particularly if the actor is known to be proud of his 'motor' and is willing to laugh at himself!

*(Enter Jim, very laid-back)*

**Jim**     *(Offhand)* Hi!

**Phil**    *(Enthusiastically)* Did you see it, then?

**Jim**     Oh . . . it's yours, then?

**Phil**    Yeah, beautiful isn't it?

**Jim**     Well, it must have been.

**Phil**    What do you mean – it must have been?

**Jim**     Well, I can see that it must have been . . . well . . . fabulous.

**Phil**    I'm talking about the new motor.

**Jim**     Um . . . yes, I know.

**Phil**    Twenty-four-valve, turbo, the lot . . . great, eh?

**Jim**       Except for the dent in the side . . .

**Phil**      Only got it this morning . . . *The what!!!*

**Jim**       The dent in it – rear door: tractor, trailer, clunk, dent.

**Phil**      *(Furious)* Did you get the number?

**Jim**       Oh yeah – and the bloke's looking up and down the road for the owner – I said I'd pop in and see if the owner was in here.

**Phil**      *(Starts to get up)* I'm going to take his wheels off and shove them . . .

**Jim**       Now then, it's OK.

**Phil**      What do you mean, it's OK – he's ruined my new motor! I've only had it *(looks at watch)* 38 minutes . . . *38 minutes!!*

**Jim**       He said it's OK – it was his fault and he'd get it put right in the next couple of days.

**Phil**      But that's not good enough!

**Jim**       You won't get any better.

**Phil**      But he's ruined a brand-new car!!

**Jim**       The way you drive, he only beat you to it.

**Phil**      But it will never be the same.

**Jim**       It will be as good as new.

**Phil**      But it won't be 'new', will it?

**Jim**       But it isn't new anymore, anyway, is it? You drove it here – it's already got a bit of dirt on it and it's raining – it's not like it was in the showroom.

**Phil**      And this bloke said he'd put it right?

**Jim**     He said he'd put it back *(country accent)* like 'the day it were born'.

**Phil**    If only we could all do that!

### Questions you might like to think about . . .

- Is pride always wrong?
- When God saw what he had made and proclaimed it 'good', was that pride?
- When does 'looking after' our material possessions become 'pride'?

In John 3:1-8 Jesus talks of being 'born again' . . .

- In practical terms, what bearing does that have upon the events in our lives before were born again?
- What does being born of 'water' mean – why did Jesus use that expression?

The questions relating to 'Sorry, Lord' may also be relevant.

# Did you know?
# Did you care?
## (World mission)

*Trying to get a congregation interested in matters outside the walls of the church building is one of the biggest jobs of any church leadership, but unless we begin to care about people, we shall never complete the job of telling the whole world about Jesus. Some of it comes back to the fact that we are so preoccupied with what's going on in our own backyard that we are incapable of seeing outside of it . . . we haven't the time to care. And that's what the sheep and the goats were all about.*

**How you might use it . . .**

This sketch should be read quite fast, with rhythm. It should be read with the four voices spaced equally across the front of the stage.

A table with aspects of the sketch (including a Bible, a bottle of water, a copy of the *Big Issue* and a money box) could be placed in the centre, or the four readers could hold the items. An OHP with images of suffering could add to the effect. The four voices should, if possible, blend so that the general message comes across without any particular emphasis on any individual. All of us are guilty of apathy at some time or another.

| | |
|---|---|
| **1** | Did you know? |
| **2** | Know what? |
| **3** | Know who? |
| **4** | Know anything? |
| **1** | Did you know |
| **2** | that the people of Malawi |
| **3** | speak 14 different languages |

4    . . . and the Bible is only available in eight of them?

1    No I didn't.

2    I don't care.

3    They can't read anyway.

4    It doesn't matter.

     *(Pause)*

1    Did you know

2    that there are roughly

3    seven Bibles

4    in every American household?

1    I didn't.

2    I don't care.

3    They don't read them anyway.

4    Couldn't they send some of them to Malawi?

     *(Pause)*

1    Did you know

2    that 700 people in Gubissa in Ethiopia

3    relied on one muddy spring for all their water

4    until someone gave them a 40,000 litre tank to collect rainwater?

1    That's nice.

**2**    Good.

**3**    Great.

**4**    What's it got to do with me?

*(Pause)*

**1**    Did you know

**2**    that there are many thousands of families in this country

**3**    who rely upon others for food because every penny they get

**4**    goes on keeping a roof over their heads?

**1**    They should get a job.

**2**    I bought a *Big Issue.*

**3**    It's the Government's job.

**4**    What's it got to do with me?

*(Pause)*

**1**    On the Judgement Day

**2**    all the sheep and all the goats were standing before the throne

**3**    and a voice said,

**4**    'Who knew about Malawi's language problems?

**1**    Who knew about the water problems of Gubissa?

**2**    Who knew about the struggling families of Britain

**3**    and did something to help?'

**4**    A few of the sheep came forward

1    but the goats tried to hide.

2    The voice said,

3    'Who was too busy?

4    Who thought it was nice that someone else had helped?

1    Who made suggestions that others could help?

2    Who didn't care?

3    Who didn't care?

4    Who knew but didn't care?'

*(Pause)*

1    Jesus said,

2    'I tell you the truth,

3    whatever you did for the least

4    of these brothers of mine,

1    you did it for me.'

*(Pause)*

2    *(Slower)* You knew

3    *(Slower)* and you cared.

**Questions you might like to think about . . .**

Read the parable of the sheep and goats in Matthew 25:31-46.

- Is the idea of sending Bibles from America to Malawi so silly?

- What stops us caring? What starts us caring?

- Was Jesus more interested in people's spiritual than physical well being?

- How can we tell what people actually need, as opposed to what we think they need?

The questions relating to 'Salt 'n' light' may also be relevant.

# Marriage . . . so what?

1 Lyrics of 'I would do anything for love' – Number 1 Single in 1995 by Meatloaf
2 'Declaration of Intent' – a poem by Steve Turner
3 A genuine letter in *Woman's Weekly* agony column (Jan 1995)
4 Verses from Genesis, Exodus, Jeremiah and Mark

*This sketch is simply the reading of four approaches to marriage placed alongside each other: a song of good intentions, a poem of sad reflections, a confused letter of desperation and a series of verses as to how it was meant to be.*

### How you might use it . . .

This sketch could be staged in a similar way to the previous sketch, with one difference. Here, four different voices would provide a contrast for the parts which would enable continuity of their reading. Whilst the lyrics of 'I would do anything for love' may be unfamiliar to some, an expressive reading of them would indicate the passion of the lyricist. 'Declaration of Intent' needs to be read in the slightly bitter tone of someone who has been rejected and is trying to rationalise their feelings. The *Woman's Weekly* letter is one of pain and a desire for an answer and requires a voice that is full of questions. The verses are read 'straight' – the aim to be the backdrop into which the other thoughts are fed.

1    I would do anything for love,
      I'd run right into hell and back.
      I would do anything for love,
      I'd never lie to you and that's a fact.

2    She said she'd love me for eternity
      but managed to reduce it to eight months for good behaviour.

3    We've been married for three years now
      and to begin with we were very much in love.

4    For this reason a man will leave his father and mother
      and be united to his wife and they will become one flesh.

**1**    I would do anything for love
and I'll be there until the final act.
I would do anything for love
and I'll take a vow and sign a pact.

**3**    I still feel the same feelings towards David
but his feelings have changed.

**2**    She said we fitted like a hand in a glove
but then the hot weather came and such accessories weren't needed.

**4**    Do not commit adultery.

**3**    David spends much less time with me and is not so loving.
A long time ago he stopped saying, 'I love you', unless I said it first
and now he doesn't even respond.

**1**    Maybe I'm crazy,
but it's crazy and it's true.
I know you can save me,
no one else can save me now but you.

**4**    Marry, and have sons and daughters,
find wives for your sons and give your daughters in marriage
so that they, too, may have sons and daughters.

**2**    She said the future was ours
but the deeds were made out in her name.

**3**    I asked him if he loved me
and he's said he doesn't know what love is.

**2**    She said I was the only one who understood completely
and then she left me
and said that she knew I'd understand completely.

**1**    I would do anything for love.
I would do anything for love
but I won't do that,
I won't do that.

**3**    Surely it can't be right to stay together for other people?
Surely love is the point of being together?

**4**    What God has joined together
let man not separate.

**Questions you might like to think about . . .**

- Is marriage important today? Why?

- What are the key ingredients that make a marriage work?

- Is it possible to guarantee that a marriage will work? How?

- If a 'full' marriage consists of love, sex and a marriage certificate, what happens if one of these is missing?

# THE RESURRECTION

# He's not here!

*Two people are looking in the empty tomb – they might be disciples – it doesn't really matter. They briefly discuss the reasons as to why it's empty and then they see something . . . someone! This can be performed on its own, or with 'He's here!'*

**How you might use it . . .**

This sketch is a short and simple introduction to the resurrection. It requires no props and no costumes – two ordinary people are trying to explain the empty tomb. The point at which they both look and see the risen Jesus and how long they look for needs careful timing.

**A**    He's not here.

**B**    What do you mean, he's not here?

**A**    Like I said – he's not here.

**B**    Well, he should be.

**A**    Well, he isn't.

**B**    All right, who's nicked him?

**A**    Don't be daft – no one's nicked him or didn't you see the two-ton boulder and the SAS guard out there yesterday?

**B**    So if no one's nicked him, how did he get out?

*(Pause)*

**A**    He could've pushed the stone away . . . OK, silly idea.

**B**    He could've dug a tunnel . . . yep, silly.

**A**    Well – if he didn't push it, or dig a tunnel . . .

**B**    . . . and no one's nicked him . . .

**A**     . . . then *where is he*?

**B**     Um.

**A**     So where is he?

*(Pause)*

*They stop and both stare at the same point (person), open-mouthed. After about 5 seconds, they drop to their knees.*

*After a further 5 seconds they exit (to the back) shouting 'He's alive', 'We've seen him', etc.*

### Questions you might like to think about . . .

- Could any of the 'explanations' of the resurrection actually explain it? If not, why not?
- Why was Jesus' body missing?
- In what ways was Jesus' resurrection body different to the pre-resurrection one?
- Why is the resurrection so important to the Christian faith?
- Is it simply a miracle, alongside all the other miracles Jesus did?
- Is it literally important or symbolically important?

1 Corinthians 15:12-58 talks more about these questions.

# He's here!

*Trying to understand what it really means when we say that Jesus is with us is really hard – especially when we talk about 'when two or three are gathered in his name'. So what does it mean when we say 'He's here'? This sketch can complement 'He's not here!' or be performed on its own.*

**How you might use it . . .**

This is a straightforward conversation between two people about the reality and implications of Jesus' promise to be with us. Whilst the conversation is primarily set in a 'church' context, how the characters are placed is open to the specific location. They could stand at the front facing the audience or hold a face-to-face conversation across a desk or could even be standing in the audience whilst having the conversation. As this sketch aims to show the idea of Jesus' presence with us, the closer the action can be to the audience, the better!


**A**    *(Looks around)* He's here!

**B**    What do you mean, he's here?

**A**    Like I said – he's here.

**B**    *(Sarcastically)* Well – there's lots of people here – so he must be – Who?

**A**    Him.

**B**    Oh . . . *(Nods or points heavenwards)* him.

**A**    No . . . not *(Nods or points heavenwards)* but . . . *(Points generally around)* . . . that's the point.

**B**    What's the point?

**A**    He said, 'Where two or three are gathered together in my name . . .

**B**    there I will be.' Yeah, I know that, so what's the problem?

**A**   Well, there's more than two or three here, so where is he?

**B**   Um . . . er . . .

**A**   If what he said is true – why can't I see him?

**B**   Ah, well, that's easy . . . there are loads of twos and threes meeting and if all of them should see him, then it would get very confusing.

**A**   So where is he?

**B**   Here.

**A**   But where . . . here? I mean *(Grabs a 'cupful' of air)* – have I got him?

**B**   Don't be daft!

*(Pause)*

**A**   Well, you tell me then where he is.

**B**   Here! Everywhere!!

**A**   So it's a bit like that song.

**B**   What song?

**A**   You know . . . 'Love is all around', 'I feel it in my fingers, I feel it in my toes'.

**B**   *(Tired)* If it helps you – then think it like that.

*(Pause)*

**A**   Look – if he is everywhere that two or three get together, then that means he's here, right?

**B**   Right.

**A**   And if he's here, then, like the song says, I should be able to feel him in my fingers, my toes – and everything, right?

**B**    Right.

**A**    So why can't I?

*(Pause)*

**B**    Maybe you've got to look for him – you know, in order to experience love, you've got to be able to learn to love.

**A**    It's the bit about him telling us we needed 'eyes to see'.

**B**    Exactly.

*(Pause)*

**A**    Funny, though.

**B**    What is?

**A**    I never came to church expecting to see him.

**B**    What did you expect to see?

**A**    People, really.

**B**    What sort of people?

**A**    Happy people – knowing what's going on in life. They're just like me most of the time but the more I see of them, the more I see someone else.

**B**    Who?

**A**    Him.

**B**    Him?

**A**    Yeah – told you he was here.

**Questions you might like to think about . . .**

Jesus said in Matthew 18:20, 'For where two or three come together in my name, there am I with them.'

- In what sense is he there?
- How can he be there – and everywhere else at the same time?
- If Jesus went back to heaven to be with his Father (see Acts 1:9-11) how can he be here with us?
- If Jesus is there when two or three are gathered in his name, what about the rest of the time?
- Are there times when Jesus isn't there?
- Is it a case of us wanting to be near him – or wanting him to be near us – or both?

The questions relating to 'The Body of Christ' may also be relevant.

# The case of the rumoured resurrection

*This 'play' was written for a youth group to perform on Easter Sunday. They wanted to present the evidence for the resurrection in the form of a courtroom drama such as is regularly seen on television. A lay magistrate made sure proceedings are more or less true to life and the ultimate decision – the verdict – is left to the congregation as members of the jury.*

## How you might use it . . .

This play is set in a courtroom and something of the formality is intended to come over in the script. If used in church, the pulpit will usually double for a witness box and the only other props would be some tables and chairs. If no pulpit is available, then a witness box can be constructed from a table, laid on its side and covered with a plain blanket. To achieve the right height, the table can be raised up by balancing it on boxes – but beware of enthusiastic witnesses who wish to hold on to or bang the witness box!

## The Cast

Courtroom staff: Usher, Judge, Prosecution Counsel, Defence Counsel.
Witnesses: Soldier, Peter, John, Mary, Thomas.

The Judge should, if possible, be played by someone highly respected who can deliver the lines with appropriate gravitas. He or she should sit in as big a chair as possible behind a large table with a gavel and a number of books piled on it. If possible, they should dress in a gown and wig, both of which can be hired at a reasonable cost.

The Usher should also, if possible, be dressed in a gown and should be chosen for their ability to be busy and assume an officious nature!

The Counsels are the two parts that require most preparation as they need to be able to react to the script rather than simply read it. They would benefit from the right costume including sharp suits, gowns and wigs, and are best positioned facing each other across desks on either side, but in front of, the judge. Again, piles of what appear to be weighty legal tomes on the desk add to the effect. The casting of actors depends on their ability to assume the caricature of the average TV barrister.

### The Witnesses

As this play is set in a contemporary context, the witnesses can be dressed in modern clothes, emphasising the ordinary nature of the people involved in the original story. The Soldier would benefit from some form of army fatigues and should have a smart and efficient appearance. Peter is the rough and ready, slightly unkempt fisherman, who could arrive either with fishing rod (or net) or (even better) a full set of oilskins and sou'wester. John, on the other hand, is more studious, and should be dressed in a jumper and blazer. Mary can be flamboyant and colourful and Thomas is as down to earth as possible – dressed similar to Peter in many ways (but without the fishing gear!).

### The Play

The play consists of two parts, the prosecution case and the defence case. The charge is that Christians ('the friends of Jesus') are guilty of fraud in claiming the resurrection. The aim of the prosecution is to show the resurrection has no hard evidence to back it up, citing traditional explanations for the absence of the body. The defence case refutes these explanations and shows that the eyewitness accounts in the Bible were given by people who were as surprised by events as anyone. The judge sums up the case and invites the audience, as the jury, to decide on two crucial questions – whether the resurrection actually happened and the ramifications if it did.

There is a gap between the two halves which requires filling as the play itself is not long enough to warrant refreshments at that point. It is suggested that a song be used, either performed or prerecorded in conjunction with a video. Videos such as 'Jesus of Nazareth' provide opportunities (copyright permitting) for those with video editing facilities which could show aspects of the crucifixion and resurrection.

If this is used as an evangelistic opportunity, it is a good idea to offer refreshments together with further information about the Christian faith such as tracts and a bookstall. Books such as *Who Moved the Stone?* by Frank Morrison are essential further reading!

### Use of an OHP

A considerable amount of information is conveyed during the play and it is useful to have an OHP to project aspects of the case as well as the relevant Gospel accounts of the resurrection. It is quite important that the OHP is positioned as close to the centre of proceedings as possible in order that the attention of the audience is not distracted by the words that appear. It may be that pauses are required at some point to draw attention to the OHP and allow time for crucial passages to be read. It is left to the performers to decide at which points this might be required.

*Part 1*

**Usher**  *(Speaking from the back of the 'courtroom')* Court rise – stand up everyone.

*(Enter Judge. Counsel for prosecution and defence stand.)*

**Judge**  *(Sits)* Please sit down. This court is now in session. We shall hear a charge being made and a defence against that charge. Who is bringing the charge?

**Prosecution**  *(Stands)* I do, my Lord.

**Judge**  What is the charge?

*(Acetate 1 – Words of charge appears: 'That the friends of Jesus Christ are guilty of fraud in claiming that he has risen from the dead')*

**Prosecution**  The charge is this: 'That the friends of Jesus Christ are guilty of fraud in claiming that he has risen from the dead'. This is a lie that his friends have been repeating until it has been believed by millions even though what they claim is simply a rumour, based on gossip. My Lord, we shall present witnesses who will show that there is absolutely no evidence that this man rose from the dead. We shall show that there are a number of good explanations for the disappearance of a body from a tomb and that those who claim the resurrection took place are unreliable and make fantastic claims that they cannot prove.

**Judge**  Thank you – and who appears for the defence?

*(Acetate 1 off)*

**Defence**  *(Stands)* I do, my Lord. The case for the defence, my Lord, is based on reliable eye-witness reports and on sworn statements taken around the time of the events. Another aspect of our case is the change in individual lives brought about by an event that the individuals concerned neither witnessed themselves nor fully understand but which has changed them and everything they stand for.

*(The Judge stands and faces the congregation)*
*(Acetate 1 – Words of charge reappears)*

**Judge**    Will everyone please stand.

**Usher**    All rise in Court.

**Judge**    Ladies and Gentlemen of the jury. You must decide whether what you hear proves the charge of fraud against the friends of Jesus Christ. This is a serious allegation and it will be a decision you and no one else can take. So listen carefully. Please sit down. Mr Prosecutor, present your case.

*(Acetate 2 – The three aspects of the case for the prosecution:*
*1 – The witnesses are unreliable*
*2 – Other explanations*
*3 – The presence of the resurrected man)*

**Prosecution**    *(Stands)* Our case, my Lord, relies on three basic facts: First – the witnesses of this event are notoriously unreliable. Second – there are other perfectly reasonable explanations for this event. Third – if this man has risen from the dead, we demand his presence in this courtroom today. *(Acetate 2 off)* So, firstly – the witnesses to the story put about by the friends of Jesus Christ are notoriously unreliable. Women, for example, who cannot be . . .

**Defence**    *(Stands)* Objection!

**Judge**    Mr Prosecutor, why are women unreliable witnesses?

**Prosecution**    In the society in which this happened, women were second-class citizens.

**Judge**    Does that make them unreliable witnesses?

**Prosecution**    No one would take any notice of what they said.

**Judge**    This court recognises that everyone's testimony must be heard, including women's.

**Prosecution**    Well, if my Lord pleases, we will accept the validity of the women's testimony but not of others involved, such as fishermen, prostitutes and others that . . .

**Defence**    *(Stands)* Objection!

**Judge**    Mr Prosecutor, a court must accept witnesses, whoever they are and whatever their status in life. Can you prove that the ability to tell the truth is any different in a dustman rather than a lawyer?

**Prosecution**    No, my Lord.

**Judge**    Then we shall proceed with evidence presented by people of any status in society of either sex. Please proceed.

**Prosecution**    Thank you, my Lord. The second strand of our case is that there are other perfectly reasonable explanations for the event. My Lord, what appears to be death is not always so – there are well-documented cases of people who have appeared to have died only to be revived when taken to the cool air of the mortuary. I would cite the case of a doctor's wife in England in the mid 1990s declared dead by her GP only to be found breathing as she was being taken to the mortuary. Jesus Christ was on the cross for a mere six hours, a very short time compared to the many days that it took some criminals to die. We assert that Jesus Christ did not die – he fainted and then revived in the tomb. As someone who had grown up as a carpenter, he was an immensely strong man who would have easily been able to force his way out of the tomb and pretend to his friends that he had come back to life. This, my Lord, is a perfectly reasonable explanation of the events although an equally convincing explanation presents itself: namely, Jesus Christ did die on the cross, but his friends came and removed the body during the Sabbath Day and have been telling people since that he has come back to life. I will now call my first witness, Roman Guard, Flavius . . .

**Usher**    Flavius to the witness box, please.

*(Flavius, a Roman Guard goes into the witness box)*

**Prosecution**  Your name and occupation, please.

**Guard**  Flavius, Soldier in the Imperial Roman Army, Jerusalem Garrison.

**Prosecution**  Please tell us what happened on the Sabbath night in question.

**Guard**  It's all a bit embarrassing really. We came on duty on Friday and were told to report for special guard orders. Apparently there was some Jewish nutter who had been executed and the local religious bigwigs were in a bit of a state because this nutter had said he would come back from the dead. They'd gone to the big boss, Pilate, and asked whether we could make sure that nothing happened, like the nutter's friends nicking the body or something.

**Prosecution**  I see, so what happened?

**Guard**  Well, we were so . . . er . . . tired by the Saturday night that . . . um . . . we nodded off.

**Prosecution**  And?

**Guard**  When we woke up, the nutter's mates were hotfooting it out of the garden with the body. By the time we had come to, it was too late.

**Prosecution**  Did you look for them?

**Guard**  Of course, but we're not locals. They had disappeared into the back streets and that was that.

**Prosecution**  Thank you. There, my Lord, I think we have a perfectly plausible version of events.

**Judge**  Before you move on, does the Defence want to cross-examine the witness?

**Defence**  *(Stands)* We certainly do, my Lord. *(To the soldier)* Are Roman soldiers well-paid?

**Guard**    Not as much as we'd like.

**Defence**    So a little extra always helps?

**Guard**    Certainly does.

**Defence**    Even when it is from the Jewish authorities to help spread a lie?

*(Acetate 3 – Matthew 28:11-15)*

**Guard**    Um . . . I don't know what you're getting at.

**Defence**    I am getting at the fact that the Jewish authorities told you to tell this story about the so-called nutter's friends stealing the body, didn't they?

**Guard**    *(Pauses and then answers quietly)* Yes.

**Defence**    I'm sorry, I didn't quite hear you. Let us get this straight – the friends did not take the body, did they?

**Guard**    *(Quietly)* No.

*(Acetate 3 off)*

**Defence**    *(Pauses)* Flavius, were you present at the execution of the prisoner?

**Guard**    Yes.

**Defence**    Did one of your colleagues pierce the body of the prisoner with a spear?

**Guard**    Yes.

**Defence**    And was there a flow of blood and water from the wound?

**Guard**    Yes, there was.

**Defence**    Does the presence of blood and water in these circumstances indicate death?

**Guard**   Yes, it does.

**Defence**   My Lord, this is well documented in the statement signed by John. *(To the Soldier)* So would you say that you saw the said Jesus Christ dead?

**Guard**   Yes.

**Defence**   No more questions, my Lord.

**Judge**   You may leave the stand, Flavius. *(Soldier leaves)* Prosecution, continue.

*(Acetate 2 – the three aspects of the case for the prosecution)*

**Prosecution**   The final part of our case is, my Lord, the most convincing. We are talking about people who had a lot to lose: friends of a man who they believed to be someone special, someone for whom they have given up livelihoods to follow, someone who was a fraud.

**Defence**   *(Stands, calmly)* Objection!

**Judge**   Yes?

**Defence**   The person in question can only be named to be a fraud if the prosecution proves their case.

**Judge**   Objection sustained. *(To the prosecution)* You have brought this case and you know that until proved, the charge is an allegation only.

**Prosecution**   Very well, my Lord. The evidence for the resurrection of Jesus Christ relies on the witness statements of people who claim to have seen this man alive after he had been crucified. The case against them is simply this: they, and millions like them since, believe this man to have come back to life because they want it to have happened, because they have put so much trust in this man that his death shows them for what they are – failures. They have deluded themselves that he has come back to life when the simple facts of life say that when a man is dead — he is dead. No one can cheat death, and these deluded people believe that because Jesus did it, so can they. The case for the prosecution is this: That if this Jesus Christ came back from the dead then he must still be alive . . . we demand his presence here in the witness stand. Bring him into this courtroom: let him be here — for all of us so see him! They cannot — and everything science tells us, everything our instincts tell us, and everything in the world says that they can't do it. He's as dead as a doornail. The defence cannot produce him — and never will. The prosecution rests.

*(Acetate 2 off as Prosecutor sits down)*

**Judge**  The court will adjourn before hearing the case for the defence.

**Usher**  All rise.

*(All rise, Counsels nod to Judge who then leaves)*

### Part 2

**Usher**  *(Speaking from the back of the 'courtroom')* All rise — please stand up. *(Enter Judge. Counsel for prosecution and defence stand.)*

**Judge**  *(Sits)* The court will now hear the case for the defence. Please be seated.

**Defence**  Thank you, my Lord. The case for the defence, too, rests on three points.

*(Acetate 4 — The three aspects of the case for the defence*
*1 — No other explanation*
*2 — Reliable witnesses*
*3 — The presence of the resurrected man)*

First — there is no other explanation for the events other than to conclude that Jesus Christ did indeed rise from the dead. Second — the defence will produce reliable witnesses, to show that many sightings of this man have taken place. Third – we shall answer the demand made by the defence that we should produce this man, here, today. Regarding the first, we can prove that Jesus did die on the cross: after a flogging of such severity (many people died under it even before being crucified) to be subjected to the loss of blood from the nails and the suffocation that occurs in crucifixion, there is no doubt that the man was dead.

*(Acetate 5 – John 19:32-34)*

And here I produce a witness statement, evidence of which we have already heard, from the guard, Flavius. A clear statement that Jesus Christ was dead. We have already shown that the Guards had been paid off to tell a story that has been shown to be false.

*(Acetate 5 off)*

And so I turn to the eyewitness reports *(He holds up individual Gospel Booklets)*: Two of these were written by Matthew and John who had followed the story right from its earlier days, and one was written by Mark, believed to be in the wider circle of Jesus' friends. The other was written by a Greek doctor, researching the story with tremendous eye for detail. All of these witness statements agree on one fundamental issue: that Jesus Christ did rise from the dead. This court has already accepted that the testimony of women (which earlier courts might not have been willing to accept) is as valid as those of men. I call Mary Magdalene.

**Usher**  Mary Magdalene to the stand, Mary Magdalene, please.

*(Mary enters witness box)*

**Defence**  Mary, how did you know this man, Jesus?

**Mary**  He healed me, that's how. I was in a terrible state and seven different spirits had taken over my life. Jesus simply released me from their grip – he made me free.

**Defence**  And what happened on that morning, two days after Jesus was crucified?

**Mary**  I don't think anyone can tell you just how awful that Sabbath Day was. We had watched a totally innocent man, a dear friend, die and because of the rules about the Sabbath we had to wait until the Sunday morning to anoint his body. *(Acetate 6 – Mark 16:1-8)* In addition, we were worried because we knew they'd rolled this stone in front of the grave and we would somehow have to move it.

**Defence**  So what happened when you got there?

**Mary**  We looked up and the stone was already gone. We went inside to see if the grave had been robbed and there was this man in there who told us that Jesus wasn't there.

**Defence**  What did he say?

**Mary**  He said, 'Don't be alarmed. You are looking for Jesus, who was crucified. He has risen, he is not here. See the place where they laid him.'

**Defence**  Then what happened?

*(Acetate 6 replaced by Acetate 7 – John 20:14-18)*

**Mary**  Well – I was very confused: I'd come to anoint a dead body – which wasn't there and now there was someone telling me he'd come back to life. It was terribly confusing and I was in a right state, and as I was wandering back through the garden, trying to make head or tail of it, I met this bloke – I assumed he was the gardener or something.

**Defence**  What did he say to you?

**Mary**  He asked me who I was looking for. I thought he might know what had happened, so I asked him. And then he said one word . . . my name, 'Mary', just like that – nothing else. And I suddenly realised it was him, Jesus.

**Defence**   And what did you say?

**Mary**   What else could I say? I just melted into tears and said, 'Teacher' and fell down at his feet. He told me that I musn't cling on to him. That was so hard to do – I was so afraid I'd lose him for good but I then sprinted back to where I knew all the others were and started shouting that he was alive and that I'd seen him.

**Defence**   Did they believe you?

**Mary**   I'm not really sure. But then they all ran off to see for themselves.

**Defence**   Mary, is it possible you might have imagined all of this? I mean, you didn't want him to die, did you?

**Mary**   Look – I didn't want him to die, sure, but equally, I never imagined I'd see him alive again. He was dead – I'd watched him die – and I expected him to stay dead. I know what I saw. I know that I felt the feet of a person – not a ghost. I know that I spoke to him – and he's alive. There is absolutely no doubt about it.

*(Acetate 7 off)*

**Defence**   Thank you, Mary, you may stand down. I would now like to call another eyewitness, Peter.

**Usher**   Simon Peter to the witness stand, Simon Peter.

*(Mary leaves witness box, Peter enters witness box)*

**Defence**   Peter, how did you feel that morning?

**Peter**   Like the others – devastated – and me more than most.

**Defence**   Why's that?

**Peter**   I was the one who had said I would never desert him and then I lied three times to avoid being arrested with him.

**Defence**    So what happened when Mary arrived with the story that she'd seen him?

**Peter**    Maybe I thought she was nuts and that the emotion of it all had got to her, and then I thought – what if it's true? I mean, Jesus had spent three years doing things that, well, you don't normally see and I suppose I thought – maybe *something* has happened.

**Defence**    What, in particular?

**Peter**    I don't know – but I thought I'd go and have a look, anyway.

*(Acetate 8 – Luke 24:10-12)*

**Defence**    And what happened when you got there?

**Peter**    Well, nothing really. We got there and the tomb was empty. The clothes were in a mess and he was gone.

**Defence**    Did you see anyone?

**Peter**    No.

**Defence**    So what happened?

**Peter**    I went home, trying to work out what was going on.

**Judge**    *(To prosecution)* Do you wish to cross-examine this witness?

**Prosecution**    Yes, my Lord. *(Acetate 8 replaced by Acetate 9 – Luke 24:12; John 20:6-7)* Peter, your testimony, recorded by Luke, the Greek doctor, says that you saw the strips of linen but nothing else, and yet, the witness statement of John, who was there with you in the tomb, states quite clearly that the strips of linen were there but that the cloth around the head was separate. Can you explain this discrepancy in the evidence?

**Peter**    The testimony that Luke wrote down was just as I had remembered it. John obviously remembered it differently.

These statements were only written down because John and I were getting old and we wanted the story to be told after we had died.

**Prosecution**   But what about the discrepancy?

**Peter**   It was the most important day in the history of the universe and John and I remember it differently – it must have been forty years later when it was written down. I remembered it one way, he in another. All I know is that the body was gone, not exactly how the grave clothes remained.

**Prosecution**   Thank you, no further questions.

**Judge**   *(To defence)* Do you wish to question this witness further?

**Defence**   Yes, my Lord. Peter, did you actually see Jesus alive?

*(Acetate 9 replaced by Acetate 10 – Luke 24:13, 33, 34)*

**Peter**   Oh yes, I saw him later on that day and then we had breakfast with him a few days later.

**Defence**   Pardon?

**Peter**   Sorry. We had been told to go back up North to where we had met Jesus in the first place, to Galilee where we had been fishermen. We had decided whilst we were waiting for Jesus that we would go fishing.

*(Acetate 10 replaced by Acetate 11 – John 21:2-14)*

**Defence**   And how did you get on?

**Peter**   Lousy, absolutely lousy. All night we were at it but not a nibble. And then, just as the sun was coming up we heard this voice, 'Have you caught anything?' We shouted back, 'No', and then the voice said, 'Try the right side of the boat'.

**Defence**   What was your reaction?

**Peter**     Well, to be honest, what a smart Alec! Here we are, up all night, nothing to show for it and here's this twit on the shore telling us how to fish. But then we thought, 'Why not, we've tried everything else'; and then, bingo! We counted them – 153 whoppers! And then I knew it.

**Defence**     Knew what?

**Peter**     There is only one person who could have known that there were fish there – Jesus. I was off like Linford Christie on a good day! I shouted, 'It's the Lord!' and dived off the boat. The others weren't too impressed at me leaving them to bring the catch in but I didn't care: if Jesus was there, that's where I wanted to be! And when we got ashore, he'd got breakfast ready, and then we talked: talked about what he wanted me to do now.

**Defence**     And what was that?

**Peter**     Look after the others, keep the group together, simply to love them.

**Defence**     Peter, Jesus was your best friend for three years . . . is it possible you could have imagined seeing him, because you wanted to?

**Peter**     No! How many ghosts have you had breakfast with? How many ghosts have you had conversations with? Of course I didn't imagine it. Jesus was as real as you are – and he still is. I'll do anything for him – like he did every-thing for me.

**Defence**     Anything?

**Peter**     Definitely.

**Defence**     No further questions, Peter, you may step down. *(Peter leaves witness box)* Call Thomas *(Thomas enters witness box as Acetate 11 is replaced by 12 – John 20:19-29)* Thomas, you knew Jesus for three years, along with all of the other so-called disciples, didn't you?

**Thomas**     That's true.

**Defence**    And yet you didn't believe them when they said they had seen Jesus alive?

**Thomas**     No. I'm a down-to-earth sort of bloke who likes a bit of evidence. So when they said they'd seen him, I thought, 'Yeah, right!, they wish!' I said I'd only believe if I could touch his hands and feet.

**Defence**    And did you?

**Thomas**     Yeah, a week later. We were having a conflab about what to do, where to go; and, frankly, I was not really interested because it was all, 'If you'd seen him, Tom, then you'd know . . .' That sort of thing. And then, there he was – the door was locked – no one heard him come in – he was just there.

**Defence**    And?

**Thomas**     And I realised what an idiot I'd been: I should have believed him when he'd said he would come back to life. I should have trusted the others. But now I believe – it is all true – I'm lucky, because I saw it. Jesus said that it was even better that there were people who would believe it even though they hadn't seen it.

**Defence**    Thank you, Thomas, no further questions. *(Thomas leaves witness box)*

               *(Acetate 12 replaced by Acetate 13 – Luke 24:13-16, 28-31)*

**Defence**    My Lord, we also have the statements of some travellers on their way to Emmaus the same day: They met with Jesus on the road and ate with him, before returning to the rest of the group. *(Holds up a sheaf of papers)* We also have statements from other friends: John, one of the inner circle, who was with Peter at the empty tomb, in the locked room, and out on the lake. We have the statement of Saul, also known as Paul, who met with Jesus on a journey to Damascus, as well as statements that over 500 people saw this man alive.

**Judge**  Before we proceed with these statements, is there anything the prosecution would like to say.

**Prosecution**  Yes there is, my Lord. The defence can produce all of these statements, but they all are from friends of the man concerned. Do they have any independent witnesses?

*(Acetate 13 off)*

**Defence**  Yes, my Lord. May I draw your attention to the witness statement of one Josephus. Josephus was a historian of the Jewish nation during the time of the Roman occupation and the life of Jesus. His book, *Antiquities*, is an invaluable and respected resource for those who study this era. He was neither an acquaintance nor a follower of Jesus Christ, and his testimony is as follows *(OHP 14 – Josephus):*

*And there arose about this time* [he means Pilate's time as governor, AD 26-36] *Jesus, a wise man if indeed one should call him a man. For he was the performer of astonishing deeds, a teacher of those who are happy to receive the truth. He won over many Jews and also many Greeks. He was the Christ. And when Pilate had condemned him to the cross at the instigation of our own leaders, those who had loved him at first did not give up. For he appeared to them on the third day alive again, as the holy prophets had foretold and had said many other wonderful things about him. And still to this day the race of Christians, so called after him, has not died out. (Antiquities 18.3.3)*

I reiterate: '*And when Pilate had condemned him to the cross at the instigation of our own leaders, those who had loved him at first did not give up. For he appeared to them on the third day alive again . . .*' This statement came from a witness independent to those we have seen; he reports the incident we are discussing as *fact* and not as *supposition.*

123

My Lord, we could go on producing witnesses but there are other facts that this court should consider: *(Acetate 4 – the defence case – reappears)* Firstly, we argue that the followers of Jesus such as Peter, Thomas, and others would be not prepared to go all the way to death for something they knew to be a lie. Secondly, there are millions, even billions of people in the world today, still willing to swear that this man did, indeed, come back to life. In the intervening 2000 years, no one has been able to show it up as a lie.

My Lord, the prosecution concluded their case by challenging the defence to produce the man, Jesus, here, today, in this court. I cannot produce a body, here, today, but I can produce hundreds, thousands, millions of witnesses. All are willing to testify to the fact that this man is alive, that he was taken up into heaven and that the Holy Spirit of God came in his place ten days later in a dramatic and miraculous way. These witnesses will testify to the fact the this same Spirit lives in every follower of Jesus Christ from that day to this.

In conclusion, the resurrection did take place – there is no other possible explanation for the incredible events of that Sunday morning.

The resurrection did take place – there are literally hundreds of witnesses who have testified to the fact that this event took place.

The resurrection did take place – there are millions of people alive today who will testify to the fact that this man, Jesus Christ, not only was resurrected on the Sunday morning in question but is alive today and active in the lives of his followers through his Spirit.

I cannot produce him physically before this court but I can say that he is *literally* with us now in the hearts and lives of his followers. I rest my case.

*(The defence sits down as Acetate 1 – Words of charge – is projected)*

**Judge**    Members of the Jury, you have heard the arguments of the prosecution: Firstly, that the friends of Jesus Christ stole his body. Secondly, that he did not die on the cross, but was revived in the cold of the tomb. But do not forget the fact that the guards were bribed to give false evidence and that proof of Christ's death was seen at the execution in the blood and water that flowed from the wound caused by the spear.

From the defence you have heard many eye-witness accounts of the resurrection. Do not be alarmed by slight variations: A court always suspects collusion if witness accounts are identical. These accounts relate not to one sighting, but many. They relate to a large number of people sighting this man alive. These facts are important.

As to the claim that this man, Jesus Christ, is present in this room, here, today – this is for you to decide. The argument of the defence is that this man lives in the lives of his followers. You must look into the lives of his followers and decide if this claim is true. There are two crucial matters for you to decide:

*(Acetate 1 replaced by Acetate 15: Crucial question 1 – Did the resurrection take place? Yes or No)*

If you decide that the resurrection did not happen then you accept that Jesus Christ was a liar and a fraud because he promised that it would happen. If he lied, then none of his teaching is valid.

If, on the other hand, you decide that the resurrection did take place then a second crucial question must be answered:

*(Acetate 15 replaced by Acetate 16: Crucial question 2 – If the resurrection happened, what does it mean?)*

If this event did take place then you must decide its significance. A man has died, claiming to take the sin of the world with him to the grave. The claim has been made that he has returned from the grave. If the evidence has shown that this man returned from the grave then you cannot escape the further question as to its significance in the lives of those who follow this man.

And, finally, and most important of all, you must decide whether the resurrection should have a significance in your own life. The decision is yours, and yours alone. You will leave this court to consider your verdict.

**Usher**   Court rise – please stand.

*(The Judge and Counsel stand, bow to each other and depart)*

### Questions you might like to think about . . .

- What are the possible verdicts?
- Is an 'open' verdict (i.e. 'we can never know') a legitimate answer? If not, why not?
- The witnesses portrayed here (Mary, Peter, Thomas and John) saw the resurrected Jesus with their own eyes – do you think there was ever any doubt in their minds?
- Do we have faith in the resurrection, or the one who was resurrected? Is there a difference or a connection?
- Is faith about a 100 per cent certainty, or the balance of belief?
- Hebrews 11:1 defines faith and goes on to discuss faith throughout the Bible: Is faith a way of life, or a trust in facts?
- When we say a Creed, what are we saying?
- Is it important/possible/necessary to believe in every single aspect of the Nicene Creed?
- Is it important/possible/necessary to understand all of the matters we say we believe in?

The questions relating to 'He's here!' and 'He's not here!' may also be relevant.